Southern Poets

Edited By Georgia Harris-Love

First published in Great Britain in 2017 by:

Young Writers
Remus House
Coltsfoot Drive
Peterborough
PE2 9BF
Telephone: 01733 890066
Website: www.youngwriters.co.uk

All Rights Reserved
Book Design by Spencer Hart
© Copyright Contributors 2017
SB ISBN 978-1-78820-867-3
Printed and bound in the UK by BookPrintingUK
Website: www.bookprintinguk.com
YB0319AZ

Foreword

Dear Reader,

Welcome to this book packed full of feathery, furry and scaly friends!

Young Writers' Poetry Safari competition was specifically designed for 5-7 year-olds as a fun introduction to poetry and as a way to think about the world of animals. They could write about pets, exotic animals, dinosaurs and you'll even find a few crazy creatures that have never been seen before! From this starting point, the poems could be as simple or as elaborate as the writer wanted, using imagination and descriptive language.

Given the young age of the entrants, we have tried to include as many poems as possible. Here at Young Writers we believe that seeing their work in print will inspire a love of reading and writing and give these young poets the confidence to develop their skills in the future. Poetry is a wonderful way to introduce young children to the idea of rhyme and rhythm and helps learning and development of communication, language and literacy skills.

These young poets have used their creative writing abilities, sentence structure skills, thoughtful vocabulary and most importantly, their imaginations, to make their poems and the animals within them come alive. I hope you enjoy reading them as much as we have.

Georgia Harris-Love

Contents

Breakwater Academy, Newhaven

Kallie Jean Burtenshaw (6)	1
Adele Susan Olivia Mack (5)	2
Alexis Rose Pal (6)	3

Compton & Up Marden CE School, Compton

Dylan Dyssell (7)	4
Madeleine Wakelin (7)	5
Henry Milne (6)	6
Tabitha Grace Townsend (5)	7
Amy Phillips (6)	8
Marcia Dicken (5)	9
Jonty Lomas (7)	10
Cameron Bosson (6)	11
Grace Kinder (5)	12

Heene CE Primary School, Worthing

Abigail Standing (6)	13
Edie Sellwood (7)	14
Lily Evans (6)	16
Faith Louise Young (7)	17
Katie Grimwade (7)	18
Marian Delmo (6)	19
Ronnie Ewen-Smith (7)	20
Julian Glowacki (6)	22
Skyler Austin-Prior (6)	23
Mabel Eastty (7)	24
Marlie Pelling (6)	25
Penelope Bluebell Read (6)	26
Daisy-May Winson (7)	27
Polly Cooper (7)	28

Hailey Wood (6)	29
Daniel Spencer (6)	30
Phoenix Scott (7)	31
Ollie Cager (6)	32
Borbala O'Donnell (7)	33
Summer Hunnisett (6)	34
Ben Van Staaden (7)	35
Oliver Matthew Groves (7)	36
Natalia Olivia Campbell (6)	37
Brooke Denyer (7)	38
Regina-Fae O'Brien (6)	39
Lucas Fuller (6)	40
Seth Elliott (6)	41
Jazmin Hill (7)	42
Riley Hunt (7)	43

Queen's College Junior School, Taunton

Liv Williams (6)	44
Lily Colman (6)	45
Máté Mayer (6)	46
Thomas Taylor (6)	47
Sam Zomorrodian (7)	48
Mayu Renee Yoshimasu (7)	49
Ben Weeks (6)	50
Sophie Smy (7)	51
Adam Tariq Evanson Smyth (7)	52
Francesca Smith (7)	53
Lottie Still (6)	54
Keanu Campbell (6)	55
Oliver Jebjerg (7)	56

Silverdale Primary School, St Leonards-On-Sea

Grace-Mae Wright (7)	57
Lyla Page (6)	58
Delilah Jacobs (7)	59
Zoe Dodd (7)	60
Star Mayley (6)	61
Izzy Taylor (7)	62
Miley Tanner (7), Zac Lawrence (6) & Jude Drinkwater (7)	63
Rabia Genc (7)	64
Summer Rose Jones (6)	65
Sienna Barry (7)	66
Abdah Rilwan (7)	67
Lilly Davidson (7)	68
Sophie Wadbrook (6)	69
Jack Wilkins (6)	70
Ashby Roberts (6)	71
Amy Witcombe (7)	72
Toby O'Donoghue (7)	73
Laila Evans (7)	74
Rian Henry Thomas Porter (7)	75
Chloe Deeprose-Mitchell (7)	76
Makayla Hawkins (7)	77
Willem James Driver (7)	78
Saéanna May Doré (6)	79
Jude Healey (7)	80
Zack Robert David Lydon-James (7)	81
Amelia Pryor (6)	82
Henry Brown (6)	83
Maisie Card (7)	84
Shay Rixon (7)	85
Alfie Cleaver (7)	86
Sophie Harbour (6)	87
Luke Roberts (6)	88
Freya Rose Treen (7)	89
Anya Barry (6)	90
Lexie Tuppenney (7)	91
Bethany Maurice (7)	92
Ollie Wright (7)	93
Theo Kennedy (6)	94

St Leonards CE Primary Academy, St Leonards-On-Sea

Jack Corrigan (7)	95
Charlie Ryan (7)	96
Cadence Amy Shearer (6)	97
Finley Peoples (6)	98
Hollie Watford (7)	99
Lily Beth Diett (6)	100
Ashton Wright (7)	101
Jack Edward Smoothy (7)	102
Monica Rousey Liu (6)	103
Annie-Rose McGowan (6)	104
Lily Hawes (6)	105
Alistair Spiers (7)	106
Edward Green (6)	107
Brooke Madison Bailey Wells (6)	108
Anthony Tapp (7)	109
Pheobe Olivia Williams (6)	110
Kit Mackinnon Pearce (6)	111
Denis Ryslink (6)	112
Myles John Edwards (7)	113
Harrison Barrett (7)	114
Maya Haji (6)	115
Aidan Hepworth (7)	116
Jaeger Kenzie Smith (6)	117
Joseph Bourne (6)	118

St Mark's CE Primary School, Hadlow Down

George Lawson (6)	119
Eleya Presler-Jones (7)	120
Scott Langley (6)	121
Molly Burden (7)	122
Sophie Imogen Lilliott (7)	123
Oliver Benjamin Erridge (7)	124
Jesse J A Wilkes (7)	125
Ellie Parrington (5)	126
Maxime Félicité (6)	127
Florence Shipley (7)	128
Iola Koukourakis (5)	129
Charlie Cook (5)	130
Sukie Rose Jary (5)	131

Charlotte Brown (5) 132
Maxwell Coppard (5) 133
Callum Jack Hudson-Ward (6) 134
Kirah Saige Presler-Jones (6) 135

The Erme Primary School, Ivybridge

Harry Patrick Readey (5) 136
Liam Dijkstra (6) 137
Evie Rayner (7) 138
Liam Turney (5) 139
Isla Ruby Dibben (5) 140
Robyn Hawling (6) 141
Ella Smith (6) 142
Harry Jones (5) 143

Turners Hill CE Primary School, Turners Hill

Amy Knight (5) 144
Oliver Walton (5) 145
Mally Ashok (5) 146
Isla Duff-Cole (5) 147
Hissaan Mahmood (6) 148
Dylan Brackpool (5) 149
George Connaughton (5) 150
Mylon Ashok (5) 151
Ryan Duff-Cole (5) 152

Bad Pets

I don't want a white shark,
it's too scary.
I don't want an elephant,
it's too big.
I don't want a fly,
it's too buzzy.
I don't want a rabbit,
it's too bouncy.
I don't want a wasp,
it's too stingy.
I do want a puppy,
it's perfect.

Kallie Jean Burtenshaw (6)
Breakwater Academy, Newhaven

Bad Pets

I don't want an elephant,
it's too fat.
I don't want a fly,
it's too buzzy.
I don't want a tiger,
it's too fierce.
I don't want a dog,
it's too noisy.
I do want a cat,
it's too perfect!

Adele Susan Olivia Mack (5)
Breakwater Academy, Newhaven

Bad Pets

I don't want a cat,
it's too boring.
I don't want a leopard,
it's too scary.
I don't want a dragon,
it's too dangerous.
I do want a dog,
it's perfect!

Alexis Rose Pal (6)
Breakwater Academy, Newhaven

Gasquach The Crazy Creature

My creature's colours are red, like a shooting star.
Their size is smaller than a giant's mouth.
His shape is a cube, with a massive head.
His legs are tiny, like a cat's head and legs.
They looked like a flaming, terrible robot with a lava bucket.
He feels like a spiky hedgehog.
He sounds like a loud gun.
He smells like a juicy apple.
He moves like a bouncing cheetah.
Its name is Gasquach.
Watch out for Gasquach, he might eat you.

Dylan Dyssell (7)
Compton & Up Marden CE School, Compton

Steve, My Crazy Creature

My creature's colours are brown and grey, like a silver birch tree.
He is a rat with kangaroo legs,
but his size is in-between a rabbit and a butterfly.
My creature's name is Steve.
He is very hard to find because he leaps through the night and he whistles!
The crazy thing about my creature is, he smells of fresh bananas!
Steve's favourite food is leaves from a tree in the forest.

Madeleine Wakelin (7)
Compton & Up Marden CE School, Compton

Black Spike

My creature's colour is black as soot.
Their size is tall, like a house.
His shape is an oval, like a stone.
They look like black straws, like the night sky.
He feels like the smooth wings of a butterfly.
He sounds like a storm with lightning.
He smells like an old purse.
He moves like an old and stinky giant.
Watch out for my scary Black Spike.

Henry Milne (6)
Compton & Up Marden CE School, Compton

Pipa The Magical Creature

My creature's colours are a rainbow, like a moon.
Their size is small like a mouse.
Their shape is rectangular.
They look like a dog.
They feel like a soft cat.
They sound like a chair.
They smell like poppies.
They move like a mouse.
Look out for the beautiful and fun *Pipa*.

Tabitha Grace Townsend (5)
Compton & Up Marden CE School, Compton

Cake-Ball The Magical Creature

My creature is red and brown like chocolate.
He is very small and round like a ball.
He smells like spilled milk.
He moves like a red panda.
He sounds like a crazy dog.
He feels like a small egg.
He is like a fresh cake.
He can fly, but he's very slow.
He is very fun!

Amy Phillips (6)
Compton & Up Marden CE School, Compton

Star The Magical Creature

My creature's colours are like a bear.
Her size is small, like a mouse.
Her shape is one like a panda.
She looks like a little dormouse.
She feels like a little rat.
She smells like pink perfume.
She moves like a slow snake.
Her name is Starlight.

Marcia Dicken (5)
Compton & Up Marden CE School, Compton

Spice The Crazy Creature

He is older than my grandma.
He is tall like a very tall tree.
His colour is brown.
His shape is an oval.
He feels like a straw.
He sounds like a man with a low voice.
He smells like cheese.

Jonty Lomas (7)
Compton & Up Marden CE School, Compton

Crok The Crazy Creature

His size is long.
His colour is red.
His shape is like a cuboid.
He feels hard with spikes outside.
He looks like a lizard.
He sounds like a crocodile.
He smells like a lemon.

Cameron Bosson (6)
Compton & Up Marden CE School, Compton

Starshan The Magical Creature

She is big, even bigger than a bear.
She is green, like a snake.
She feels like a pillow.
She looks like a tiger.
She sounds like a lion.
She smells like flowers.

Grace Kinder (5)
Compton & Up Marden CE School, Compton

Snake

I am as dark as a bat.
I am as quick as a cheetah.
I am as long as a cobra.
I am light as a feather.
Keep me vicious.
Keep me warm.
Slither, slither!
Get me food.
Slither, slither!
Get me water.
Get me prey.
Slither, slither!
Can you teach me?
Get me a treat.
Slither, slither!
Do not poke me or I will bite you!

Abigail Standing (6)
Heene CE Primary School, Worthing

Tiger

Tiger, tiger
under the long legs there is the
d
r
i
p
p
i
n
g
blood from his last prey.

In the dark of the wood
There was…
A stealthy creature.
Creeping past, hunting his…

Prey.
Roar! It's
A-a-a-a-
Tiger
Run, it's gaining on us. Run!
It's as big as London! A-a-a-a
big one. Run!
Edie Sellwood (7)
Heene CE Primary School, Worthing

The Dog

The warm and fluffy creature, the dog
hiding in its kennel.
Chewing the bone on his throne.
Smelling, chasing cats
All around the garden.
After chasing for many hours
he gets his own way.
Pouncing on the cat
he pushes the cat off the wall,
it takes a terrible fall off the wall.
The cat's owner is terribly cross with the dog.

Lily Evans (6)
Heene CE Primary School, Worthing

Panda

I hear a *crunch, crunch* through the dark forest.
I hear an animal screaming.
It smells like dusty mud.
It sounds like a growl and I walk even closer.
It looks like black and white stripes,
black, googly eyes, a hairy body, a black shiny nose.
It sounds like bamboo being eaten by a panda!

Faith Louise Young (7)
Heene CE Primary School, Worthing

The Unicorn

Unicorn, unicorn,
happy as candy as he skips along happily,
through the swishing grass
into his unicorn place
To have a race,
to see who would come first.
He runs like thunder.
He's fast, so watch out for him!
He leaps around so happy!
The unicorn is the winner.

Katie Grimwade (7)
Heene CE Primary School, Worthing

Peacock

Up, up the elegant, grand bird flies.
The wings float up into the blue, blue sky.
A wonderful bird with incredible, soft feathers, that shine in the sunlight, so colourful and bright.
Feathers as soft, as fluffy as clouds and its legs are as short as a bunny's.

Marian Delmo (6)
Heene CE Primary School, Worthing

Poisonous Snake

The
snake
is
sssssslithering...
to
you
in
the
dark
of
the
night.
Snake,
snake,
poisonous
snake
is
sssssslithering

at
you!
Sssss!
Ronnie Ewen-Smith (7)
Heene CE Primary School, Worthing

Chameleon

Chameleon, chameleon,
turn as blue as the midnight sky.
Chameleon, chameleon
turn as yellow as the golden sun.
Chameleon, chameleon,
turn as green as the leaves and the grass.
Chameleon, chameleon,
turn as blue as the daylight sky.

Julian Glowacki (6)
Heene CE Primary School, Worthing

Cobra

Sheep, pow!
A strike of venom.
Sheep, pow!
A strike of venom.
Sheep, wow!
Cat, pow!
A strike of venom.
Cat, pow!
A strike of venom.
Cat, wow!
Cobra, *argh!*
Pow! A strike of venom.

Skyler Austin-Prior (6)
Heene CE Primary School, Worthing

The Gorilla Peeks

Swinging from tree to tree.
The gorilla peeks through the leaves and looks for juicy apples to eat.
Gorilla, gorilla!
Run, run from the snakes!
Run, run!
You silly gorilla.
You are frightening the birds.

Mabel Eastty (7)
Heene CE Primary School, Worthing

Tiger, Tiger

Tiger, tiger sniffs his prey,
you are all furry.
Tiger, tiger your claws are sweet
like a cute little kitten.
It was thundering and
Tiger got wet.
He played outside
And got wet again.

Marlie Pelling (6)
Heene CE Primary School, Worthing

The Hungry Unicorn

Unicorn, unicorn,
soft and colourful,
walks in the long, long grass.
She finds some hay,
walks away
like a gentle, soft cloud.
She walks softly back home
for her delicious dinner.

Penelope Bluebell Read (6)
Heene CE Primary School, Worthing

The Candy Cat

The candy cat, the candy cat
jumped so high on the trampoline.
The candy cat, the candy cat,
it's time for dinner.
The candy cat, the candy cat,
it's time for pudding.

Daisy-May Winson (7)
Heene CE Primary School, Worthing

Rabbit, Rabbit

Rabbit, rabbit,
pink and yellow,
runs like lightning to the carrots.
Rabbit, rabbit,
eats the
delicious, sweet,
nice,
scrummy,
yummy,
awesome
carrot.

Polly Cooper (7)
Heene CE Primary School, Worthing

Giraffe

Giraffe
Giraffe
Are you tall?
Giraffe
Giraffe
Tall like a giant.
Giraffe
Giraffe
You are beautiful.
Giraffe
Giraffe
Beautiful, like a flower.

Hailey Wood (6)
Heene CE Primary School, Worthing

Ladybird

Ladybird, ladybird.
Wave your delicate wings.
Ladybird, ladybird.
Wave your lacy wings.
Ladybird, ladybird.
Don't be scared.
Ladybird, ladybird.
Be brave.

Daniel Spencer (6)
Heene CE Primary School, Worthing

Sharky, Sharky

There was a fierce shark,
who had a house made out of electric sparks.
He liked whales
without the tails.
When he was three,
he swam in the sea
and that's me!

Phoenix Scott (7)
Heene CE Primary School, Worthing

Cool Gorilla

Cool gorilla
Swinging up a tree
Ate his banana
Swinging in the tree.
Cool gorilla swinging in a tree.
Cool gorilla swinging in a tree.
Fur as black as coal.

Ollie Cager (6)
Heene CE Primary School, Worthing

Snake

Poisonous snake,
Poisonous snake.
Run up the tree
Down the mountain
Around the rock.
Your body is scaly...
as scaly as a dragon.
Ssssss.

Borbala O'Donnell (7)
Heene CE Primary School, Worthing

Dragon, Dragon

Wake, wake dragon.
Dragon, who are you?
Teatime
Bath time
Sleep time
Teatime.
Cock-a-doodle-doo.
Dragon, dragon
Wake up.
Go to school.

Summer Hunnisett (6)
Heene CE Primary School, Worthing

Snake

Slither snake.
Oh slither snake.
As slimy as seaweed.
Slither snake.
Oh slither snake.
As shiny as water.
Slither, just slither
Under a cave.

Ben Van Staaden (7)
Heene CE Primary School, Worthing

Black Panther

Panther,
Panther
In
the
night.
blazing, shining eyes.
Pounce,
pounce on your prey.
Munch, munch - there goes your prey.

Oliver Matthew Groves (7)
Heene CE Primary School, Worthing

Scratching Cat

Scratch, scratch cat.
Just miaow, miaow cat.
Cats just miaow.
I want a cat.
Scratch, miaow, cat.
Scratch, miaow, cat.
I want a cat.

Natalia Olivia Campbell (6)
Heene CE Primary School, Worthing

Tiger

Roar! Roar! Roar!
Hungry tiger.
Teeth as sharp as a knife.
Roar! Roar!
Hungry tiger.
I love your orange stripes.

Brooke Denyer (7)
Heene CE Primary School, Worthing

Centipede

Tip, tap
Centipede
Walking up the tree.
Tip, tap
Centipede
Eating all the leaves.
Munch!

Regina-Fae O'Brien (6)
Heene CE Primary School, Worthing

Snake

The snake is slithering through the grass.
It's smooth and shiny.
It pounces on its prey.
Like a darting flash of thunder.

Lucas Fuller (6)
Heene CE Primary School, Worthing

Zebra

Zebra, zebra
Black and white.
I need to play with you.
Zebra, zebra
Black and white.
I need to talk to you.

Seth Elliott (6)
Heene CE Primary School, Worthing

Tiger, Tiger

Tiger, tiger, below the tall shiny tree.
His body is stripy and furry.
His claws are shiny and sharp.

Jazmin Hill (7)
Heene CE Primary School, Worthing

Cat

Cat
you sit on the mat
And you play in the day.
You are as soft as a bunny.

Riley Hunt (7)
Heene CE Primary School, Worthing

Dolphin

Dolphin, oh dolphin, how I love your colour.
The grey and black fins help you swim.
You swim so gracefully and elegantly as the light dims.
Your disguise makes you clever to catch your fish.
Your friendliness is strong and your sharing too.
You are the ruler of the oceans and seas.
But how I wish to see you soon and maybe I will.
Goodbye dolphin, I want to see you soon.

Liv Williams (6)
Queen's College Junior School, Taunton

Angelfish

A nice angelfish with glittering fins and beautiful skin.
It eats seaweed and crabs.
It hides away because of animals wanting to eat it.
Clean teeth and dazzling colours,
it makes rainbows all around.
It shoots out blue, pink and rainbow colours.
Purple as well and golden hairs.
It goes out in the open seas.

Lily Colman (6)
Queen's College Junior School, Taunton

The Whale

The humpback whale is spiky.
The humpback whale is quiet and fast down in the sea.
The humpback whale is angry and tall.
The humpback whale is as long as two buses.
The humpback whale is dangerous.
The humpback whale likes eating huge and small fish.
The humpback whale is stronger than a car.

Máté Mayer (6)
Queen's College Junior School, Taunton

The Small Manta Ray

The manta ray is hungry.
The manta ray is fast.
The manta ray is strong.
The manta ray is sleepy.
The manta ray is rare.
The manta ray is playful.
The manta ray is fierce.
The manta ray eats small fish.
The manta ray is blue and white
and the manta ray is me.

Thomas Taylor (6)
Queen's College Junior School, Taunton

Turtle

Sea turtles are slow.
Sea turtles hunt for food.
Sea turtles eat phytoplankton as they swim along.
Sea turtles are really awesome and cute.
Sea turtles live underwater.
Sea turtles lay eggs.
Sea turtles live in the open sea.
That's why sea turtles are important.

Sam Zomorrodian (7)
Queen's College Junior School, Taunton

Sea Turtle

The green turtle has got a black, dark eye.
It looks to see if there is danger.
When there is a mummy turtle,
it goes up, to show it has got a baby in her tummy.
It has got big, green, floppy feet swimming gently.
The turtle eats white shrimp
because it loves shrimps.

Mayu Renee Yoshimasu (7)
Queen's College Junior School, Taunton

Octopus

White spots on its tentacles.
A round, angry mouth, opening and shutting.
As it floats by, it leaves its legs out.
Catching prey, but the thing I like the most is...
They aren't normally very dangerous.
So people can touch them.

Ben Weeks (6)
Queen's College Junior School, Taunton

The Sea Turtle

The deep, dark and scary eyes,
The bumpy, hard shell for his home.
The green, patchwork skin,
The smooth fins help him swim from side to side,
Very elegantly its head sways.

Sophie Smy (7)
Queen's College Junior School, Taunton

Dolphin

The dolphin is nice and calm.
The pitch grey dolphin is harmless and fast.
The happy dolphin is eating all the cod.
What he does not know, is that a shark is right behind him!

Adam Tariq Evanson Smyth (7)
Queen's College Junior School, Taunton

Seahorses

A cute seahorse was swimming around the open oceans.
It was very funny.
It loves eating plankton.
It loves jumping up and down.
It loves to go to the middle of the sea.

Francesca Smith (7)
Queen's College Junior School, Taunton

Seahorses

Seahorses love to play,
they bump up and down.
They get tired and are hungry,
they eat zooplankton.
After they eat their food
they go to sleep.

Lottie Still (6)
Queen's College Junior School, Taunton

The Dugong

The dugong is huge and gigantic.
It eat some fish through the sea,
in the open sea.
It is massive
and huge like a car.

Keanu Campbell (6)
Queen's College Junior School, Taunton

Whale

The mouth is really big.
The tail can flap.
The eyes are blue and big.
The gigantic body glides through the sea.

Oliver Jebjerg (7)
Queen's College Junior School, Taunton

Giraffe Sense Poem

A giraffe tastes like a smooth yellow banana with lots of bruises on its skin.
It looks as light as the boiling sun shining in the clear blue sky.
When the giraffe's feet are swishing through the water,
It sounds like a waterfall gushing down into the river.
A giraffe smells like a rotten banana with mould inside.
A giraffe feels as soft as a teddy bear with lots of warm fur.

Grace-Mae Wright (7)
Silverdale Primary School, St Leonards-On-Sea

Meerkat Sense Poem

The cute, small meerkat looks like a little furry thing runs very fast.
The soft, tiny meerkat smells like the bugs they eat.
The stripy, fast meerkat feels like a fluffy ball of feathers.
The long meerkat sounds like pattering of paws clattering on the floor.
The meerkat would taste like slimy bugs.

Lyla Page (6)
Silverdale Primary School, St Leonards-On-Sea

Elephant

The elephant feels as soft as cat's fur.
The elephant sounds like thunder.
The elephant is as tall as twenty trees.
It lives in a zoo or in Africa!
The elephant likes to play in cold water.
The elephant tastes like a tree trunk.
The elephant looks like a grey gorilla.

Delilah Jacobs (7)
Silverdale Primary School, St Leonards-On-Sea

Lizard Sense Poem

A fast lizard tastes like a hard, chewy brick.
It feels like rough, scaly rooftops shaking in the breeze.
The lizard can hear a hissing sound like a snake.
It looks like two small lumps of blue and orange.
The short lizard smells like sand in the salty, blue sea.

Zoe Dodd (7)
Silverdale Primary School, St Leonards-On-Sea

Meerkat Sense Poem

The meerkat smells like fresh worms and bugs.
The meerkat touches the African sand as it runs through the desert.
The meerkat tastes slimy, like blue worms and bugs.
The meerkat looks like soft dry sand that is dusty.
The meerkat sounds squeaky, like a squirrel.

Star Mayley (6)
Silverdale Primary School, St Leonards-On-Sea

The Lonely Giraffe

The lonely giraffe is as smelly as an old grandma's hair.
The sad, lonely giraffe tastes like cold, squishy breeze.
The cheeky, sad giraffe sounds like a meerkat.
The giraffe looks like an ostrich.
The cold, lonely giraffe feels soft and squishy.

Izzy Taylor (7)
Silverdale Primary School, St Leonards-On-Sea

Giraffes

Giraffes taste like yellow, sweet bananas.
Giraffes look like cookies.
Giraffes sound very noisy.
Giraffes feel like soft, furry pom-poms.
Giraffes smell like fresh meat and soft leaves.
Giraffes feel like a furry, spotted cheetah.

Miley Tanner (7), Zac Lawrence (6) & Jude Drinkwater (7)
Silverdale Primary School, St Leonards-On-Sea

Lion

The lion roars with a fearsome sound.
Roar, roar, roar!
The lion smells as muddy as an elephant.
The lion is as soft as a kitten.
The lion looks like a fearless cheetah.
The lion tastes as meaty as a roast turkey.

Rabia Genc (7)
Silverdale Primary School, St Leonards-On-Sea

Giraffe Poem

My giraffe feels like a big, fluffy teddy bear.
My giraffe tastes like fur.
My giraffe sounds like a caterpillar chomping on the green leaves.
My giraffe looks like a tall, towering tree.
My giraffe smells like mint leaves.

Summer Rose Jones (6)
Silverdale Primary School, St Leonards-On-Sea

The Sensible Lion

The lion looks dotty, hairy and fluffy.
The lion smells like meat and lovely fresh bacon.
The lion tastes like blood.
The lion sounds like loud volcano roars.
The lion feels like a soft, fluffy teddy bear and a pillow.

Sienna Barry (7)
Silverdale Primary School, St Leonards-On-Sea

Giraffe Poem

The giraffe is as spotty as a ladybird.
The giraffe is as tall as a tall building.
Long legs, like a zebra.
Smells like mint-green leaves.
Taste like candy canes.
Quiet as a mouse.
Feels as soft as a teddy bear.

Abdah Rilwan (7)
Silverdale Primary School, St Leonards-On-Sea

Cheetah

The cheetah is as meaty as zebra.
It is as cuddly, cute and soft as a puppy.

The cheetah's roar is as loud as a tiger.
The cheetah is as spotty as a giraffe.
The cheetah is as smelly as raw meat.

Lilly Davidson (7)
Silverdale Primary School, St Leonards-On-Sea

Cheetah Sense Poem

A yellow cheetah smells like a person.
A black cheetah looks like a spotty, yellow, shiny, wet car.
It feels like a smooth, soft, wrinkly, big bed.
It tastes like a rubber ring.
Cheetahs sound like a loud bang.

Sophie Wadbrook (6)
Silverdale Primary School, St Leonards-On-Sea

Cool Lion

Lions smell like cool, fresh meat.
Lions sound like *roar, bang and roar!*
Lions looked like giant, scary monsters.
Lions taste like burnt meat.
Lions feel like a scary, fluffy ball.

Jack Wilkins (6)
Silverdale Primary School, St Leonards-On-Sea

My Cheetah Poem

The spotty cheetah feels soft as yellow wool.
The cheetah tastes as hairy as a lion's mane.
He sounds as fast as a motorbike.
He looks like a yellow and black banana.
The cheetah smells like a chilli.

Ashby Roberts (6)
Silverdale Primary School, St Leonards-On-Sea

Snake Sense Poem

The meerkat looks golden on its arms and white on its tummy.
The meerkat squeaks like a mouse.
Meerkats taste like mint and ice cream.
Meerkats touch everything in their way.
Meerkats smell like mud pie.

Amy Witcombe (7)
Silverdale Primary School, St Leonards-On-Sea

Cheetah

The yellow and brown cheetah looks as cute as a lion.
The cute cheetah smells like fish.
The cheetah tastes like a chocolate biscuit.
The cheetah is as soft as a dog.
The cheetah is as fast as a car.

Toby O'Donoghue (7)
Silverdale Primary School, St Leonards-On-Sea

My Hyena

Hyenas taste like chocolate, squishy marshmallows.
Hyenas smell like horrible, disgusting meat.
Hyenas look like a hot chocolate bar.
Hyenas sound like evil witches.
Hyenas feel like rough popcorn.

Laila Evans (7)
Silverdale Primary School, St Leonards-On-Sea

Cheetah

The cheetah is as smelly as a sweaty foot.
The cheetah looks as spotty as a ladybird.
The cheetah sounds as loud as thunder.
The cheetah tastes as nice as meat.
The cheetah is as fluffy as a bear.

Rian Henry Thomas Porter (7)
Silverdale Primary School, St Leonards-On-Sea

Leopard

The leopard is as smelly as a hyena.
The leopard tastes like a piece of meat.
The leopard is as soft as a lion's mane.
The leopard is as loud as a lion.
The leopard looks as scary as a tiger.

Chloe Deeprose-Mitchell (7)
Silverdale Primary School, St Leonards-On-Sea

The Spotty Giraffe

Giraffes taste like yellow, sweet bananas.
Giraffes look like chocolate chip cookies.
Giraffes sound very noisy.
Giraffes feel like soft, furry bears.
They smell like fresh meat and soft leaves.

Makayla Hawkins (7)
Silverdale Primary School, St Leonards-On-Sea

Cheetah Sense Poem

The cheetah smells like a sweating honey badger.
The cheetah tastes like smooth, honey roasted chicken.
The cheetah, he has people screaming happily.
The cheetah feels as soft as a furry bear.

Willem James Driver (7)
Silverdale Primary School, St Leonards-On-Sea

Elephant

The elephant smells as stinky as mud.
The elephant looks like a muddy puddle.
It tastes like mouldy onions.
The elephant sounds as loud as a foghorn.
It feels like smooth, old tights.

Saéanna May Doré (6)
Silverdale Primary School, St Leonards-On-Sea

Cheetah

The cheetah is one of the fastest animals in the world.
It smells like a cute and cuddly cat.
The cheetah tastes like a spotty black and yellow animal.
It sounds like a very fast car.

Jude Healey (7)
Silverdale Primary School, St Leonards-On-Sea

Cheetah

A cheetah is spotty as a giraffe.
Cheetahs smell like a dirty boy.
Cheetahs feel like a teddy bear.
It might taste like meat.
A cheetah's claws are as sharp as a knife

Zack Robert David Lydon-James (7)
Silverdale Primary School, St Leonards-On-Sea

Elephant

An elephant is as fat as a bale of hay.
An elephant is a kind of meat.
Elephants are as smelly as mud.
An elephant eats like a child.
An elephant smells as muddy as a buffalo.

Amelia Pryor (6)
Silverdale Primary School, St Leonards-On-Sea

Hyena

A hyena feels as fluffy as a kitten.
The hyena tastes like a turkey.
A hyena looks like a cheetah.
A hyena smells like perfume.
It sounds like a dog barking.

Henry Brown (6)
Silverdale Primary School, St Leonards-On-Sea

The Silly Giraffe

The giraffe looks like a chocolate chip cookie.
The giraffe smells like blue cheese.
The giraffe tastes like a spiky hedgehog.
The giraffe feels like a cushion.

Maisie Card (7)
Silverdale Primary School, St Leonards-On-Sea

Cheetah

A cheetah is as fast as a racing car,
Soft as a dog.
Its growl is as loud as a revving engine.
A cheetah smells like bear fur.
It tastes like furry meat.

Shay Rixon (7)
Silverdale Primary School, St Leonards-On-Sea

Cheetah

A cheetah is as fast as a flash.
A cheetah's claws are very long.
A cheetah's tail is as long as a snake.
A cheetah's fur is as furry as a lion.

Alfie Cleaver (7)
Silverdale Primary School, St Leonards-On-Sea

Meerkat

The meerkat looks skinny as a pencil.
The meerkat tastes like dried meat.
The meerkat feels like a teddy bear.
The meerkat sounds like a baby fox howling.

Sophie Harbour (6)
Silverdale Primary School, St Leonards-On-Sea

Snake

The snake smells like gooey slime.
Snakes taste like boiled eggs.
The snake hears meerkats underground.
The snake feels likes slime and ooze.

Luke Roberts (6)
Silverdale Primary School, St Leonards-On-Sea

Cheetah

The cheetah has a nose as pink as candyfloss.
The cheetah feels like a soft, fluffy, yellow banana.
The cheetah smells like a chocolate chip cake.

Freya Rose Treen (7)
Silverdale Primary School, St Leonards-On-Sea

Cheetah

My cheetah is as spotty as a giraffe.
My cheetah is as fast as a lion.
My cheetah is as quick as lightning!
Growling like an angry lion.

Anya Barry (6)
Silverdale Primary School, St Leonards-On-Sea

My Snake Sense Poem

The snake smells like fresh dirt.
The orange snake touches the light green grass.
It moves slowly as it glides over the bumpy sand.

Lexie Tuppenney (7)
Silverdale Primary School, St Leonards-On-Sea

Giraffe

A giraffe looks like a chocolate chip cookie with a gold crust.
Giraffes taste like heaven.
A giraffe feels like a rabbit.

Bethany Maurice (7)
Silverdale Primary School, St Leonards-On-Sea

The Cheeky Cheetah

Cheetahs taste like brown chocolate.
The cheetah smells like old, stinky poo.
Cheetahs look like a walking banana.

Ollie Wright (7)
Silverdale Primary School, St Leonards-On-Sea

Monkey

Monkeys sound like a very large bang!
Monkeys look like chocolate chip cookies.
Monkeys smell like bananas.

Theo Kennedy (6)
Silverdale Primary School, St Leonards-On-Sea

Wild Dog's Poem

Wild dogs pounce on their prey
on the golden and sandy beach.
They run through the hot, sunny and orange
desert in the day.
When the sun sets
the wild dog settles down in its
underground burrow.
Wild dogs smell like dogs
when they are dirty.
Wild dogs kill their prey
by pouncing on them.
Their enemies are the prey they eat.
The wild dogs are very scary
and soft and cosy.
What an amazing sense of smell it has.

Jack Corrigan (7)
St Leonards CE Primary Academy, St Leonards-On-Sea

Orangutan Poem

Orangutans like to swing off brown, green and vast trees
to fetch yellow, squishy and cold bananas.
They are very cute, sweet and very fluffy animals.
Orangutans are just like humans, but very fluffy.
They live in zoos or forests.
Orangutans are very good at climbing trees.
They like to go on top of green, curly and vast trees.
Orangutans love eating yellow bananas.
Orangutans are absolutely brilliant at climbing trees.

Charlie Ryan (7)
St Leonards CE Primary Academy, St Leonards-On-Sea

Zebras

Zebras can run fast like cute little horses.
They eat yummy and delicious grass.
The zebra is cute and lovely!
Fast like a tiny and cute leopard.
What an adorable, cute and little zebra!
Zebras are cute and adorable, like a baby leopard.
Zebras have black and white stripes on their bodies.

Cadence Amy Shearer (6)
St Leonards CE Primary Academy, St Leonards-On-Sea

Vulture

A vulture flew through white clouds.
The vulture went to sneak on its prey.
The vulture flew through the cold breeze.
A vulture is mean.
How mean is that?
The vulture was mean and ate a
dead orange fox.
A vulture ate a dead monkey.
As evil as a T-rex.
They are so mean!

Finley Peoples (6)
St Leonards CE Primary Academy, St Leonards-On-Sea

Leopards

Leopards like to eat prey.
All is quiet.
When they come on the sunny days, all the animals are quiet.
Leopards are as fast as a cheetah when they pounce.
They are cute when they're babies,
but grown-up leopards are fierce!
What scary animals they are!
Beware of their teeth!

Hollie Watford (7)
St Leonards CE Primary Academy, St Leonards-On-Sea

Unusual Leopards

Leopards run with speed in the long, swaying grass.
A hungry leopard eats a deadly vulture.
Leopard is as mean as a hyena.
A fierce leopard is waiting for you.
A leopard is camouflaged by the grass.
Leopards don't like water.
A leopard is very fast.

Lily Beth Diett (6)
St Leonards CE Primary Academy, St Leonards-On-Sea

Naughty Gorillas

Leaping quietly through the strong trees,
Black gorillas are on their way!
They love hiding and leaping on other
ferocious animals!
They are as brave as Grace Darling.
Underneath green vines and leaves
Gorillas are sleeping quietly.

Ashton Wright (7)
St Leonards CE Primary Academy, St Leonards-On-Sea

Crocodile Dog

I live in a house down a beautiful Lane.
He loves to eat meat.
He likes to go to the park.
When he goes to the park he barks and barks and barks!
He loves women.
He likes chewing his dog food.
He likes having his hair brushed.

Jack Edward Smoothy (7)
St Leonards CE Primary Academy, St Leonards-On-Sea

Untitled

K ind kitten, helps people.
I s like wet ice cubes melting.
T rees covering the cute kitten.
T rees covering the cute kitten.
E njoying milk.
N aughty kitten scratching faces.

Monica Rousey Liu (6)
St Leonards CE Primary Academy, St Leonards-On-Sea

Snakes

Snakes slither and slide through the long, swaying grass.
Most snakes live in woods and the wild.
Snakes eat rats.
In the summer, snakes peel their skin.
Some snakes have green bodies and black stripes.
Most snakes hiss!

Annie-Rose McGowan (6)
St Leonards CE Primary Academy, St Leonards-On-Sea

Cheetahs

Cheetahs run fast to catch their prey.
They go into their den when it is too hot.
Daddy cheetahs like to run.
Mummy cheetahs hide the babies from getting eaten.
They hunt the zebra.
They hide in grass.

Lily Hawes (6)
St Leonards CE Primary Academy, St Leonards-On-Sea

Cheetahs

Cheetahs are as fast as leopards
when they pounce on their poor prey.
They are camouflaged in the swaying grass.
They sprint to catch their prey.
Cheetahs are the fastest animals
in the noisy jungle.

Alistair Spiers (7)
St Leonards CE Primary Academy, St Leonards-On-Sea

Gorilla

Gorillas swing on the branches to get their prey.
No one knows when the gorilla is going to attack.
Right when the gorilla is on the top of the branch
it pounces on its prey!
In the trees a gorilla hides.

Edward Green (6)
St Leonards CE Primary Academy, St Leonards-On-Sea

Snake

Snakes slither all through the long, green, swishy grass.
Children and adults don't know the snake is out there.
The snake is camouflaged in the grass for protection.
Some snakes eat baby snakes.

Brooke Madison Bailey Wells (6)
St Leonards CE Primary Academy, St Leonards-On-Sea

Monkey Band

M onkeys are here,
O ne monkey band.
N oisy like a lion,
K icking the annoying drums.
E lectric guitars are buzzing,
Y elling at the animals.

Anthony Tapp (7)
St Leonards CE Primary Academy, St Leonards-On-Sea

Kitten

K itty claws, really sharp.
I tching to play with me!
T ickling me with its feet.
T oo fluffy for me!
E xciting play!
N aughty little kitty!

Pheobe Olivia Williams (6)
St Leonards CE Primary Academy, St Leonards-On-Sea

The Naughty Python

P lanning and cunning,
Y ellow and sharply coloured,
T ry me, naughty fellow.
H asty and scaly,
O range and scaly,
N early black and yellow.

Kit Mackinnon Pearce (6)
St Leonards CE Primary Academy, St Leonards-On-Sea

Leopard

L ikes running.
E ats meat.
O n the hunt.
P ouncing.
A nice piece of meat.
R unning through the grass.
D eep in the jungle.

Denis Ryslink (6)
St Leonards CE Primary Academy, St Leonards-On-Sea

Cheetahs

Cheetahs are as fast as a flash.
The roaring cheetah ate an antelope.
Cheetahs are camouflaged with their spots.
Cheetahs have lots of spots.
Cheetahs are fluffier than us.

Myles John Edwards (7)
St Leonards CE Primary Academy, St Leonards-On-Sea

Tiger

T errifying, fast or slow? Who knows?
I n the jungle hunting for more meat.
G iant jaws are orange.
E xcellent hearing.
R oaring on the go.

Harrison Barrett (7)
St Leonards CE Primary Academy, St Leonards-On-Sea

Zebra

Zebras run like a brown horse.
The black and white zebras run like cheetahs.
The zebra stands in the swaying grass, eating the plants.

Maya Haji (6)
St Leonards CE Primary Academy, St Leonards-On-Sea

Vulture

The vulture is as fierce as a vampire.
The vulture is very dark.
The vulture is giant.
The vulture is pecking.

Aidan Hepworth (7)
St Leonards CE Primary Academy, St Leonards-On-Sea

The Cat

The cat is cute as a baby.
The cat is as stripy as a clown's trousers.
The cat is as tall as a squirrel.

Jaeger Kenzie Smith (6)
St Leonards CE Primary Academy, St Leonards-On-Sea

Fish

Fishy fish,
I see a fish flashing.
See the fish swimming.
Seaweed is his home.

Joseph Bourne (6)
St Leonards CE Primary Academy, St Leonards-On-Sea

Miranda The Giranda

Miranda, a girander, was out for a walk one day,
She'd had a little sleep and now she wanted some bugs to eat.
There were some hunters who wanted her to pay,
So they tracked her and sent her to England to stay.
She moved to Longleat Safari Park and found some friends to play,
but she missed the rainforest and wanted to go home someday.
She met a little boy called George, who helped her run away
and put her on a plane, said goodbye and she gave him a lick
to say thank you before she flew away.

George Lawson (6)
St Mark's CE Primary School, Hadlow Down

Midnight The Adventurous Kitten

My kitten is as black as ink.
Her sandpaper tongue is pink.
Midnight's sister is called Starbright.
She has excellent eyesight.
Scramble, chase, play and climb,
fast kittens run all the time.
We cuddle and she gives us kisses,
but sometimes, when grumpy, she hisses.
Jumping and climbing with her claws,
but always gentle with her paws.
Midnight is only eight weeks old,
a baby still and uncontrolled.

Eleya Presler-Jones (7)
St Mark's CE Primary School, Hadlow Down

Dragon Lion

One little Dragon Lion eating a snack at urban jump,
went on a trampoline and landed with a bump.
A little Dragon Lion sucking up sweets,
got dizzy from all the treats!
One little Dragon Lion drank all his mum's coffee
then he went flying away, like a bee.
One little Dragon Lion off to B&Q,
he was bursting for the loo
and had a great big poo.

Scott Langley (6)
St Mark's CE Primary School, Hadlow Down

My Pet

I have a pet called Zakk
with two front legs and one at the back.
He's funny,
loves honey,
and me tickling his tummy.
He's hairy,
he's scary
and he loves to swim in dairy.
Everyone thinks he's bad,
but he is actually a good lad.
I so love my pet Zakk,
with two front legs and one at the back.

Molly Burden (7)
St Mark's CE Primary School, Hadlow Down

Jasmine The Elephant

Jasmine the elephant is big and grey,
she likes to spray water and eat plants all day.
Her trunk is long and she has big feet,
she flaps her ears in the heat.
Jasmine loves to dance and juggle
but sometimes finds it quite a struggle.
She loves playing in the sun
and thinks Africa is so much fun.

Sophie Imogen Lilliott (7)
St Mark's CE Primary School, Hadlow Down

Four Animals

Droskygin is four creatures,
Dragon, dinosaur, donkey and penguin.
He likes making sculptures,
Like plastic trees for eating.

On the moon he collects butterflies,
Where he lives all alone.
His imagination at night brings them to life,
But in the daytime they turn back to stone.

Oliver Benjamin Erridge (7)
St Mark's CE Primary School, Hadlow Down

Wonky Donkey

Eddy the donkey
Only had three legs
So he was wonky.
He was a smart dresser
And played honky-tonky
On his piano.
A magic piano
That could play by itself.
What a naughty fellow.
I thought it was Eddy.
I said, 'Hello!'

Jesse J A Wilkes (7)
St Mark's CE Primary School, Hadlow Down

My Rabbit

I have a toy rabbit,
her name is Rabbit.
My rabbit is soft and grey,
my bunny says, 'Hey.'
She has a pink nose
and big, fluffy toes.
My rabbit jumps high
and she says goodbye.

Ellie Parrington (5)
St Mark's CE Primary School, Hadlow Down

Lion

I'm a lion.
I'm a sneaky lion.
I hide in the grass
under the hot, hot sun.
I'm ready to pounce.
I'm ready to fight.
My big, sharp teeth
are ready to bite.

Maxime Félicité (6)
St Mark's CE Primary School, Hadlow Down

My Little Turtle

Turtle Wertle having eggs.
Turtle Wertle swimming with her eggs.
Turtle Wertle swimming away, singing today.
Little turtle hopes it is pancake day.
Little turtle floats away.

Florence Shipley (7)
St Mark's CE Primary School, Hadlow Down

Our Dog

Our dog makes me happy.
He has big, soft ears
and brown eyes.
He is really good at playing ball
and is never cold
when he swims in a pool.

Iola Koukourakis (5)
St Mark's CE Primary School, Hadlow Down

The Frog Poem

Frogs are green and slimy,
They hop all day and swim.
They sit on lily pads.
Frogs have super, sticky tongues,
that helps them catch the flies.

Charlie Cook (5)
St Mark's CE Primary School, Hadlow Down

If I Had A Horse

If I had a horse
I would ride it of course!
I would feed him some hay
and I would put him in the field to play.
He would be as calm as a cat.

Sukie Rose Jary (5)
St Mark's CE Primary School, Hadlow Down

Starblazer The Red Kangaroo

Starblazer was a big, red kangaroo and she loved to jump and sing all day. She carried her joey in her pouch and sang him a lullaby along the way.

Charlotte Brown (5)
St Mark's CE Primary School, Hadlow Down

Tiger

Can he really run fast?
How does he do things?
It's a tiger with a silly head,
who is friendly.

Maxwell Coppard (5)
St Mark's CE Primary School, Hadlow Down

Diplodocus

My diplodocus likes to
dance in the trees.
He likes to stomp around
and eat lots of leaves.

Callum Jack Hudson-Ward (6)
St Mark's CE Primary School, Hadlow Down

Kitten - Haiku

My kitten, Starbright,
cuddly, cheeky, balancing,
climbing green curtains.

Kirah Saige Presler-Jones (6)
St Mark's CE Primary School, Hadlow Down

The Day The Lion Came To Tea

A knock on the door,
a lion I did see.
He said, 'Can I come to tea?'
I let him in!
He drank my tea,
he drank my milk,
he didn't leave any for me!
He ate my steak
and then my cake!
He had a big fluffy mane
and he had a loud roar.
He ate all of my food
and left out my door!

Harry Patrick Readey (5)
The Erme Primary School, Ivybridge

My Tabby Cat Meowie

Meowie is a miaow cat,
She is really, really fat,
She is a tabby cat.
She purrs like a black panther,
She loves coloured plates,
She hates lion cakes.

She once bit my finger,
She once bit my toe.
I sent her to Dartmoor,
To Dartmoor she did go!

Liam Dijkstra (6)
The Erme Primary School, Ivybridge

The Wiggly Caterpillar

My caterpillar wiggles,
My caterpillar giggles.
My caterpillar is hairy,
my caterpillar is scary.
My caterpillar is green,
My caterpillar is clean.
He curls up into a ball,
But he cannot stand up tall!

Evie Rayner (7)
The Erme Primary School, Ivybridge

Nooky

Nooky is a white and orange dog.
He likes to sleep all day.
He climbs on the beds
and a big, hairy blanket
and there he stays.
Nooky likes a bone to chew,
but his favourite dinner is beef stew.

Liam Turney (5)
The Erme Primary School, Ivybridge

Stanley

He likes playing with his bone
and he likes playing with his toys.
Do you know what he likes best?
When he sees another dog he barks,
then they play together in the park!

Isla Ruby Dibben (5)
The Erme Primary School, Ivybridge

The Tiger King

Tiger, tiger shining bright
Tiger, tiger glimmering bright.
Your eyes are really, really mean!
Your eyes are like fire!
Is your meanness in your eyes?
It scares me!

Robyn Hawling (6)
The Erme Primary School, Ivybridge

Panda, Panda

Panda, panda eats bamboo.
Panda, panda, your eyes are so black.
Panda, panda you are so soft.
Panda, panda, eat so crunchy.
Panda, panda, munchy, munchy!

Ella Smith (6)
The Erme Primary School, Ivybridge

I Saw A Tiger

I saw a tiger,
I ran up a tree.
The tiger smiled up at me.
He looked like a pussy cat,
but I knew differently.
He would eat me!

Harry Jones (5)
The Erme Primary School, Ivybridge

Monkeys

Monkeys feel furry and soft.
Monkeys look brown and friendly.
Monkeys taste like bananas.
Monkeys sound like *oo oo ah ah!*
Monkeys smell of the jungle.

Amy Knight (5)
Turners Hill CE Primary School, Turners Hill

Foxes

Foxes smell stinky like an old bin.
Foxes looked like an old mop.
Foxes taste like an old ginger biscuit.
Foxes sound like dogs barking.
Foxes feel soft like a cat.

Oliver Walton (5)
Turners Hill CE Primary School, Turners Hill

Goats

Goats feel furry and tickly.
Goats smell smelly like smelly socks.
Goats look like the clouds.
Goats sound like sheep.
Goats taste like wavy, green grass.

Mally Ashok (5)
Turners Hill CE Primary School, Turners Hill

Lions

Lions smell like African grass.
Lions feel soft and strong.
Lions taste like strong meat.
Lions look like a heart beating.
Lions sound scary and fierce.

Isla Duff-Cole (5)
Turners Hill CE Primary School, Turners Hill

Dinosaurs

Dinosaurs feel bumpy and hard.
Dinosaurs look scary and huge.
Dinosaurs sound like a loud roar.
Dinosaurs smell like leaves.
Dinosaurs taste of meat.

Hissaan Mahmood (6)
Turners Hill CE Primary School, Turners Hill

Dinosaurs

Dinosaurs feel scaly.
Dinosaurs smell like meat.
Dinosaurs sound like *roar!*
Dinosaurs look spiny.
Dinosaurs taste like green leaves.

Dylan Brackpool (5)
Turners Hill CE Primary School, Turners Hill

Cheetahs

Cheetahs feel soft and warm.
Cheetahs smell like a jungle.
Cheetahs look fast and orange.
Cheetahs taste like meat.
Cheetahs sound like a big cat.

George Connaughton (5)
Turners Hill CE Primary School, Turners Hill

Snakes

Snakes feel warm and soft.
Snakes smell like meat.
Snakes taste like slime.
Snakes looked like green weeds.
Snakes sound like *hiss!*

Mylon Ashok (5)
Turners Hill CE Primary School, Turners Hill

Hedgehogs

Hedgehogs feel prickly and spiky.
Hedgehogs taste like wiggly worms.
Hedgehogs smell like a chestnut.
Hedgehogs sound like a pig.

Ryan Duff-Cole (5)
Turners Hill CE Primary School, Turners Hill

Young Writers Information

We hope you have enjoyed reading this book – and that you will continue to in the coming years.

If you're a young writer who enjoys reading and creative writing, or the parent of an enthusiastic poet or story writer, do visit our website www.youngwriters.co.uk. Here you will find free competitions, workshops and games, as well as recommended reads, a poetry glossary and our blog.

If you would like to order further copies of this book, or any of our other titles give us a call or visit **www.youngwriters.co.uk**.

Young Writers, Remus House, Coltsfoot Drive, Peterborough, PE2 9BF
(01733) 890066

info@youngwriters.co.uk